How to Stay

Married

for 50 Years

How to Stay

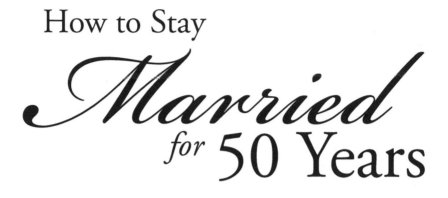

Married
for 50 Years

JOSEPH J. DOUGHERTY

To order additional copies of this book, contact:
Xlibris
1-888-795-4274
www.Xlibris.com
Orders@Xlibris.com
739621

Author: Joseph J. Dougherty

My name is Joe Dougherty. I am writing this book about my thoughts and experiences I have had in my fifty years of life with Madalyn.

Madalyn is the woman I love and I have been married to for the last fifty years. She is still the love of my life. I am dedicating this book to her. Madalyn is only nineteen years old this February by the calendar.

How to stay married for fifty years? It's not easy, man. There is only one thing to remember: Do I love this woman to actually stay for the long run?

Never say you have too many shoes. She will never have too many.

She will always have to buy a new dress for a party. Her reasoning is that everyone has already seen the others.

You will never
understand her.

Never—and I mean never—
complement another woman
on her appearance.

A compromise is when
it's your turn to speak
and she lets you.

She is always right.

Maintain separate
bank accounts.

She will ask you, "Do you think these shoes go with this dress?" Always agree. She will then change them.

What's hers is hers, and what's yours is also hers. The man always pays.

Never say anything
against her friends.

Don't complain. It will
never do any good.

Do not tell her what to do.

She will always have
the last word.

Don't complain. It will
never do any good.

Making up after a
spat is the best.

Love can be hard work.
Stay the course.

Stop what you are doing
and listen to her when
she is speaking to you.

Bring her flowers
for no reason.

Have fun and enjoy
your time together.

Never take your
troubles out on her.

Love can be hard work.
Stay the course.

Never make her cry!

Snuggle a lot. She'll love it.

When you come in and
she is singing, enjoy it.

She'll love a romantic
hot bubble bath.

Never touch her hair
after a cut and styling.

A compromise is when
you agree with her.

Always give her a special smile with an "I love you" thrown in.

Sometimes she will be crying for no reason. Give her a hug and a kiss.

Love can be hard work.
Stay the course.

Think of all the joy
she has given you.

She is the love of your life and is the most precious of all rewards. Keep her safe.

Keep romance in your
life and celebrate it.

Plan a romantic dinner
and propose to her again.

Do you remember what she was wearing when you first saw her? That will someday be on the quiz.

Fidelity at times will be difficult. Stay the course.

The thrill she gives you is never gone, but the older you get, it does slow down a bit.

Just remember that the
good old days haven't
even gotten here yet.

Happily ever after is not just in fairy tales. You can live it.

Let her know that you
love her forever.

Remember only the good
times and forget the bad.

You will never get rich
working for someone else.

If someone has to be
wrong, make it you.

Keep the music in her life.

Plan a romantic dinner for her. Love will be your guest.

She'll love a nice back rub.

Love and commitment
are hard work, so
work hard at it.

There are no easy answers
when it comes to women.

When you find Miss Right,
she will never be wrong.

Tell her that "There is no one I would want to share my life with but you."

Don't miss her birthday
without a gift.

Celebrate all your
special holidays with
love and passion.

Don't try to correct her.
(She will not be wrong.)

Never lie to her. She
will know it.

Never change the TV channel
unless you ask her first.

Love is patient and kind;
the greatest thing is love.

Absolutely never
ever strike her.

Never tell her she is wrong,
admit that you are.

Always start the new
day with a smile.

Dinner with candlelight
is very enjoyable for her.

Never criticize her. She will not see things the same way you do.

She will often change
her mind. Go with it.

When she is mad, she will have that look and sparks will fly from her eyes. BACK OFF.

You will be asked this question: Does this dress make me look fat? If you are honest and answer "Just a little," that's a big no-no. You should reply, "You look hot," or "Have you lost weight?" or something like that. Always give a compliment.

Never let her know how
sausage is made.

Keep this saying in mind:
"She who will be obeyed."
It always holds true.

She will always ask you to
put her pierced earrings in.

Try to eat breakfast together
as often as you can.

Love her is the best thing
you can do for her.

When she comes in from a hard day, ask her if you can rub her feet with lotion.

Assure her that
everything is okay when
she is feeling down.

Make her some
French toast.

Never regret a day
you have together.

Find the good in every
day with her.

Making memories is one of
the best things you can do.

Don't forget she is
always right.

Take her to dinner and
a show with dancing.

Opening a door for her is
a simple thing to do, but
it makes her feel special.

Turn off the TV at dinnertime.

Play and exercise together.

When she is not feeling
well or hurting, take
special care of her.

Try to make every day
a special day to her.

One thing she will not
tolerate is vulgar language.

Never break a promise to her.

Win over her mother
and you have it made.

Pick one of these pages
and do it every day for fifty
years and you'll get there.

Share a bottle of wine.
It makes you nicer
to each other.

Take a month off every
year and travel.

Marriage is like life,
you'll have good times
and bad times, but the
benefits are great.

Tell her often how
much you love her.

Keep God in your heart.

Gold jewelry will always
make her happy and
look good on her.

A little dog will make her happy. Let her pick it out.

Enjoy your children. They will all grow up and move on before you know it.

Always get a second
opinion when it comes
to her or your health for
major health conditions.

Hold her hand often.

Never stop loving her.

A diamond makes a great gift, especially a full carat or larger.

Even though you don't want to, go to a chick flick with her once in a while.

Always keep your car clean,
inside and out. She won't
like trash or clutter around.

Make the bed every
morning. That is helping.

Always give unexpected
kisses of love.

If it's not one thing,
it's her other.

Never interrupt her
in conversation.

Keep your opinions
to yourself even if
she asks for it.

Do what your mother always told you and pick up your mess. Do not expect her to do it.

If she is a good cook, tell her.
If not, keep it to yourself.

Never talk about your old girlfriends or keep any pictures of them around.

Compliment her hair
and makeup.

The road to a successful and
happy fifty years of marriage
is a long and hard road
with many twists and turns
but well worth the trip.

CPSIA information can be obtained
at www.ICGtesting.com
Printed in the USA
BVHW080238110119
537596BV00001B/103/P

9 781524 530228